T0365343

Lines of
REMEMBRANCE

A SHORT SERIES OF VERSE, FOR THOSE LOST IN THE GREAT WAR

JACK D. HARRISON

1663 Liberty Drive
Bloomington, IN 47403 USA
www.authorhouse.co.uk
Phone: 0800.197.4150

© 2018 Jack D. Harrison. All rights reserved.

No part of this book may be reproduced, stored in a retrieval system, or
transmitted by any means without the written permission of the author.

Published by AuthorHouse 10/22/2018

ISBN: 978-1-5462-9895-3 (sc)
ISBN: 978-1-5462-9894-6 (e)

Print information available on the last page.

Any people depicted in stock imagery provided by Getty Images are models,
and such images are being used for illustrative purposes only.
Certain stock imagery © Getty Images.

This book is printed on acid-free paper.

Because of the dynamic nature of the Internet, any web addresses or links contained in
this book may have changed since publication and may no longer be valid. The views
expressed in this work are solely those of the author and do not necessarily reflect the views
of the publisher, and the publisher hereby disclaims any responsibility for them.

authorHOUSE

TABLE OF CONTENTS

LINES OF REMEMBRANCE :
A SHORT SERIES OF VERSE, FOR THOSE LOST IN THE GREAT WAR

REMEMBRANCE OF FAMILY, FRIENDS, AND OTHERS;
NOW ONLY WITH US IN SPIRIT

A SECTION OF REMEMBRANCE, FOR BETTER TIMES PAST;

AND MORE GENERAL POETRY

DEDICATIONS

This book is dedicated first, to Mum and Dad. Sorry you're not here in person to see this;
But I know you are in Spirit.

It is also dedicated to the millions, lost during the Great War 1914-18; directly, or indirectly.
Soldiers, Sailors, Marines, Airmen, Merchant Service, Stretcher Bearers and Orderlies, Nurses, and of course, **so** many others. And those for whom, the war would never end.
Lucky to return to Blighty – then straight into Asylums; lost, within their nightmares.

And especially- to those of the 250,000 boys who raised their age to get to the Western Front.
The youngest of these was just 12 yrs. And of those, all too many were killed in action, or were 'shot at dawn', because they saw too many horrors, then simply behaved s boys their age do.
The Government and Army of the time were complicit in their death; long before their time. They also obstructed the efforts of families and their local MP, to get them back home. These boys belonged in the streets and fields of Britain, kicking a football around; not being tied to a post at dawn, or rotting in 'No-man's-land'.

Jack D. Harrison

AN ACORN'S STORY

Long ago my mother tree, grew an acorn, that was me.
I fell onto the dusty ground where I just rolled round and round.

A hungry squirrel had her eye on me,
a juicy little morsel for her tea.
She approached with the intention of wolfing me down.
Until a bigger squirrel came long, eyebrows raised with a deadly frown.

In the hubbub and kerfuffle, I rolled right under some rubble.
Dark and warm between those bricks,
Just the place I would have picked.
I sent my root to explore the soil, to anchor me firmly in place,
Where the squirrel cannot find me, I haven't left a trace.

Through the winter I rest and sleep, drinking every now and then.
As Spring creeps across the forest floor, I find myself awake again.
My shell makes an awful sound, as it cracks and falls to the ground.
I stretch young shoots to find some light, to feed me from the warm sunlight.

Beginnings of a tree that is me,
As long as those pesky birds leave me be.

I have been left alone, and a few years on I have grown.
Next to me stands a mighty Oak tree,
If I'm lucky that could be me.

The seasons gently come and go, woodland plants putting on show after show.
One Winter's day as I slumbered, I felt a hand softly stroke my back.
One man points and calls to another, "*This one would look great in the park*".
I am dug around and ripped up from the ground, from the safe place which I had found.

I am shaking and trembling along in a truck,
discarding roots and plenty of muck.
Finally, we come to a rest, and wait for it, this is the best.

Carried gently to my new home, lowered carefully into a pre-dug hole.
From where they had recently evicted an angry mole.
Space and light abound in this new home, that I have found.
This is just the place for me.

It is where I will become a mighty Ok tree.

BY TAYLOR CROWSHAW
(Published in her 2nd book 'The Tracings of My Shadow'- 2018)

LINES OF REMEMBRANCE

*A Short Series of Verse,
for Those Lost
in The Great War*

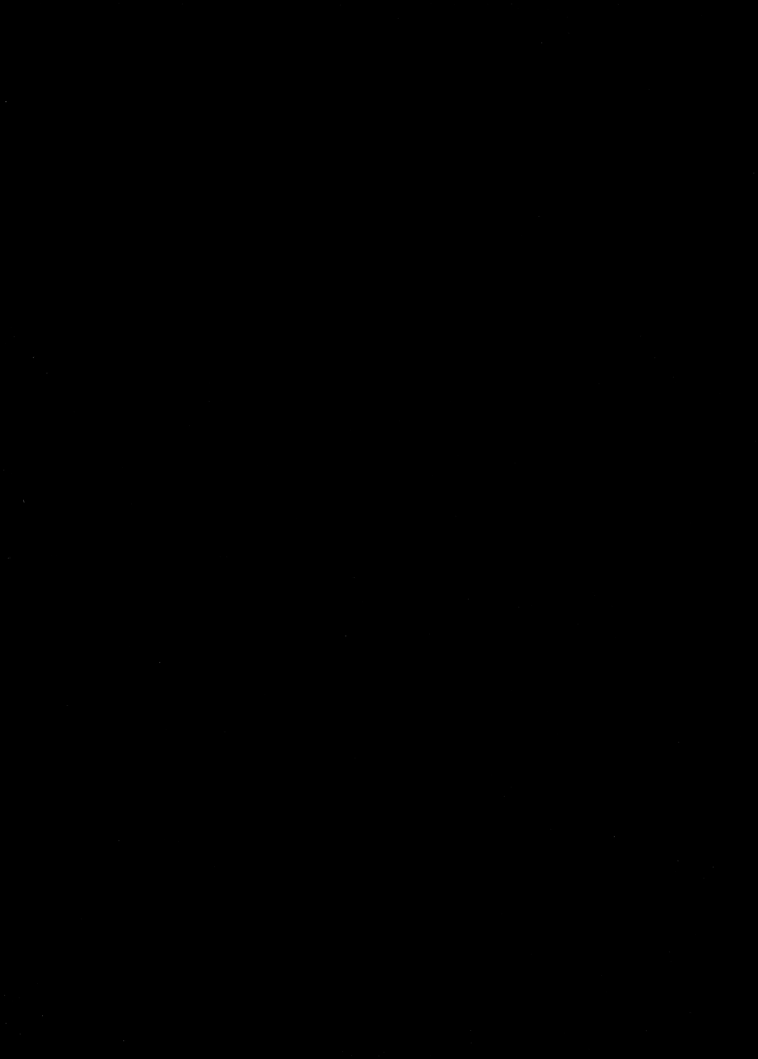

SHADOWS OF THE FALLEN

Shadows of those who remain;
standing guard over the deep red stain.
A memorial for the flower of Britain's Youth;
these sentinels remind us of the truth.

And like Sassoon who asks, "***Have you forgotten***"?
those fallen, were often parent's only begotten.
We'll NOT forget their selfless deed;
As upon their lifeblood, poppies feed.

A hundred years ago this week;
the hopes of peace, were yet still bleak.
The ideas of troops, of rest and Blighty Wounds;
or the fear of death and unfound tombs.

The youngest lost, was twelve no doubt;
he left his trench and safe redoubt.

Along with comrades, brave and true;
they gave their lives for me and you.

And so, we have our memorials;
signs of remembrance, and testimonials.
The debt of faith in them we keep;
as brave young warriors ere do sleep.

BY JACK D. HARRISON
10-07-2018

AMBULANCE TRAIN SIXTEEN

Oh coach, so clean in Summery green;
I met you once, as **'Ambulance Train 16'**.
You carried soldiers just like me;
craving smokes, and cups of tea.

I lay there bloodied in a trance;
as you bravely crossed the fields of France.
Our cries and supplications filled the night;
our wounds had given nurses such a fright.

Men whose youth were spent in sport;
now cowering at every noise's report.
Broken on the Somme, or shattered Ypres;
what horrors will their minds now keep?

Yet 'Train Sixteen', our saviour trundles on;
collecting wounded from the Front, through Rouen.
The Army Ambulance worked its deeds;
though bomb and shell, your path impedes.

"It's a blighty one for you my lad;
but poor Bertie here's, been driven mad.
The awful wounds you have to bear,
will bring so often, an unkind stare".

But more work yet, you must confront;
repatriating troops, Russia's POWs from the Eastern Front.
Doing what it always takes;
defeated and herded, from the Masurian Lakes.

Tireless nurses and bearers lost their youth;
only they will know the truth.

Safe, back in England from all the hum;
broken lives and nightmares to overcome.

And so now, as I board the 09.42;
the memories flow and I remember you.
In peacetime colours you smartly gleam;
as tired old soldiers now commute, from Cheam.

BY JACK D. HARRISON
WED 12-09-2018

THE RAF CENTENARY

In younger days. the British fought the aerial war;
with the brave men of the Royal Flying Corps.
Battling with German Aces - perforce;
before they became. 'The Royal Air Force'.

Spluttering engines announce the early dawn patrol;
as ground crew pull the chocks. and let them roll.
"Oh delicate aircraft, lean, like a Butterfly;
spitting fumes and oil, what made you fly"?

In Hunting Packs, or daring lone Reconnaissance;
allied **Camels** and **Bristols** filled the skies once.
Beware the Red Baron in his crimson Triplane;
in 'one to one' combat went their deadly dance, again.

General Smuts wrote the report, that set the scene,
to create an Air Force ne'er before seen.
A new breed of supermen sent to purge;
to battle and defeat the 'Focke-Wulf Scourge'.

Then in April 1918, The Great War brought a whole new scene;
the German's final push produced such horrors, never seen.
Von Richthofen's old Flying Circus found, a greater foe, was all around;
The RAF now ruled the Air, a force of the future I'll be bound.

The age of the Monoplane was about to come;
with new RAF Aces all brave and handsome.
They took the old baton in the Relay of the skies;
Now in their Centenary year, their chivalry ne'er dies.

And now in 2018, a boy with crisps beholds the machine;
he stands in silence, imagines himself flying, all smart and clean.
This bygone beast of endless sky;

bewitched the boy, and made him want to fly.
Let's raise a toast to those brave young men;
as Vaughan Williams' Cornet* plays, we remember them.

BY JACK D. HARRISON. NEW YEARS EVE-2017
This is a reference to Vaughan Williams' 3rd Symphony. (The Pastoral).

SNOWY PATHS

Snowy paths in Christmas Week;
lead to statues of the fallen.
Remind us of the War's first Yuletide;
and how the fighting stopped, 'Sector-wide'.

The Germans and the Allies meet;
they left their trench, to chat and greet.
Sharing smokes and carols, here or there;
as all around, the land laid bare.

The memories fade as people do;
and yet we still remember- that's true.
The snow lies virgin, crisp and bright;
just as on the trenches that Christmas night.

And as we walk upon these peacetime paths;

on Christmas Eve we recall the past.
During these Centenary Years, we take the view;
and think of the fallen, some kaki, some grey or blue.

They welcomed Granddads home again;
though millions on the battlefields remain.
And as we walk these snowy paths and think upon;
we send our own Christmas greeting - *"Tout le Monde"?*.

BY JACK D. HARRISON
CHRISTMAS EVE - 2017

POPPIES FOR LOST YOUTH

By H. Piffard

THE THIN RED LINE

Poppies in a field, in Northern France;

normally a scene of peace and romance.

But alas, the sea of crimson red;

remind us of the fallen dead.

Victims of the slaughters of 1918;

they died in such places, still only a teen.

The guns and the gas, they all did their work;

attempting their duty, not daring to shirk.

The countless spirits of soldierly youth,

do haunt the old battlefields, seeking the truth.

A hundred years of Summers went by;

was it all without reason? *"Oh why lord, oh why"?*

These crimson reminders of loss and despair,

remind us of loved ones, still lonely - out there.
We wish and we yearn, they could come back to their street.
or to fields where the poppies, caressed childhood feet.

BY JACK D. HARRISON
SUN: 29-07-2018

IS THIS A WAY TO SPEND CHRISTMAS DAY?

In seventeen Hundred and sixty six;
the Continentals taught Hessian mercenaries new tricks.
Americans crossed the Delaware over Christmas night;
and crushed the Germans, with delight

Washington's force fought on in defiance;
intent upon their rightful Independence.
The guns roared in their familiar way;
is this the way to spend Christmas Day?

And later then in 1864, as History's eye had viewed;
the Yuletide holiday they broke, in manner rude;
The Union attacked, no place for cowards there;
As 60 Northern gunboats come, the Rebel Fort Fisher was aware.

But a winter storm descended, cold;
and postponed the Yankee assault, so bold.

Confederates waited resolute, come what may;
but was this appropriate for Christmas Day?

And later still during the bloody 'Great War';
On Christmas Day towards the enemy they bore.
Our Navy Seaplanes attacked Cruxhaven;
dropped their bombs, so brave and yet craven.

And out upon the wastes of Riga. along the Eastern Front;
the Latvians attack the German Eighth, clashing in unholy shunt.
40,000 with 200 guns, sought to break invading Huns;
Is THIS a way to spend Christmas Day? No-one's idea of fun.

And yet amongst these tales of slaughter;
ties that bind nations were pulled ever tauter.
During that first Christmas of the war;
Allied and German fought no more.

Across the land owned by the French;
the troops of both sides left their trench.
From Christmas Eve until New Year;
Soldiers hailed in calls of good cheer.

Upon this last Christmas of the chivalrous ways;
they taught us how to spend Christmas Days.

BY JACK D. HARRISON
BOXING DAY-2017

UNARMED FIGHTERS

Through Sniper fire and tearing shells;
dodging holes as deep as wells.
the Stretcher Bearers left their trenches;
fighting here for King and Frenches.
Armed with only morphine and dressings;
they enter No-mans-land with Padre's blessings.

"I heard their cries, out there somewhere"
Don't worry mate, we're coming, don't despair".

The boy had been there day and night';
watching comrades cling to life, in endless fight.
But as the German shells did thud;
they lost their battle with the Passchendaele mud.

As wives and Mothers knitted socks;
and gaze at their boy's photo, with golden locks.
"Oh, when will you come back to me?
You're only twelve young years, and three".

"You left the home and ran away;
to the Western Front, raising your age, in the usual way".

Now it's just turned Dawn and something moves;
The Bearers return on booted hooves;
carrying their loads who cry and wail;
through yet another Flanders Summer Gale.
They are the Unarmed Fighters.

The Nurses work with all their might;
though deprived of rest and sleep that night;
but they did their level best.
Cutting tunics caked in mud and blood and slime;
to wounded Tummies, their pretty faces seem sublime.

For wounded troops lives, they lead the fight;
with long. long hours before respite.
their medical campaign's never done;
until the battle for lives is won.
They are also Unarmed Fighters.

A Corps of Chaplains in the field;
with words of hope they boldly wield.
For wounded soldiers amongst shell and din;
their only thought - to be brought back in.
They hope and pray all night to the Lord;
that they never visit the Dying Ward.
The Padre's work is never done;
"It's Blighty-bound for you my son".

In No-mans-land without sword or gun;
He digs two graves, watched by The Hun.
The lonely Chaplin gives Last Rites;
This scene occurred on so many nights.
They fought the good fight - unarmed. *

BY JACK D. HARRISON
15-10-2018

This is a reference to Chaplin Fr. John Lane Fox, who went out each night to bury the remains of two or three soldiers in No-man's-land; each time watched closely by German and Allied troops. He was never hindered by either side.
SEE 'WOUNDED' BY EMILY MAYHEW.
ALSO- IN UNABRIDGED AUDIOBOOK.
JDH.

REMEMBRANCE

OF

FAMILY,
FRIENDS,
AND OTHERS,
NOW WITH US
ONLY IN SPIRIT

WE WANT TO COME HOME

We watch as you stand weeping and regretting;
You keep your loyal vigil, never forgetting.
In this windswept, cold, unfriendly place;
the spears of rain assault your pretty face.
With you, in this place so bleak;
silently replying to questions,
with answers, that you seek.

But we want to come home.

And so, turning as you do, so lonely;
we always want to come too - if only.
Defeated by the Winter storm again;
I wish to see you smile, and hold your hand, in vain.

Home waits as always, on these lonely days;
The quiet fireside and cottage beckon and call you;
in the same old ways.
The things you left unsaid, bring yet more remorse;
You crave for my forgiveness, and I do my love, of course.

I've watched as you lay sleeping there, that tear upon the pillow;
dreaming of our walks on lanes, lined with herb and Willow.
Oh, I want to be there with you, and the anguish never fails;
playing football with our growing boys, and listening to their tales.
How we want to come home.

Each Christmas-time and Summer, as the parties fill the air;
you always draw back from the crowd;

and hold them- over there.
How I want to be there with you;
together, and without a care.

Yes, we all want to come home;
to the life we cannot share.

BY JACK D. HARRISON
24-09-2018

FORMER OCCUPANTS
- THE DEAD

We are the dead, not sleeping as you presume;
although it's stated on our tomb.
Though passing on, yet not to sleep;
we are your company here, to keep.

Why come you to this lonely place?
where cruel wind and hail assault your face.
You could be warm and snug inside,
whilst my fellow Spirits, roam the countryside.

We cannot speak with you, or share things now 'of late';
to touch your shoulder, make you turn, may compensate.
We fill the lonely nights with yearnings to be remember'ed,
and not just have it stated "He is dead".

Tread carefully, but you're welcome, still;
those brambles can topple you at their will.
No-one ever comes here now, no picnics in the Sun;
for it's always Winter here, and there's never any fun.

And so together here we stand;
the dead and living, hand in hand.
Like us, you roam our past abode;
those neglected buildings now forebode.

BY JACK D. HARRISON

REQUIEM FOR THE HONEY BEE

Oh furry bee where did you go?
you came this way three months ago.
The sun was warm, the weather dry;
you buzzed "hello", as you flew by.

As I was there amongst the Brambles;
full of pollen you did amble.
Then off to store your daily treasure;
filling your hive up to full measure

Oh Honey Bee, come back to me;
amongst my Brambles you're safe you'll see.
Your armed with stinger, that is true;
but yet, I love the look of you.

When sat with dog, we're ne'er alone;
kept company by your melodious drone.

The sounds of Summer now complete;
with your deep song, the birds compete.

The Blackberries form, so black and round;
as through the bloom your wings resound.
We share the space amongst spider and grub;
I watch enthralled as you rub and rub.

But as Summer Moons both wax and wane;
I wonder will you be back again.
I see you struggle until you fall;
the saddest thing to see of all.

Your Season of life so short;
there's little more for me to report.
With one last urge you, try for flight;
but t'ween lawn and path, you lose the light.

Sounds of my boyhood, you have been;
though a little scared, I've sat and seen.
Your lovely fur of black and yellow;
makes any heavy heart, ease and mellow.

And now alas we see and hear;
news of Honey Bee extinction, drawing near.
I could not bear to hear, or see;
A requiem for the Honey Bee.

BY JACK D. HARRISON
06-11-2017

NIGHT OF THE SIGNALMAN

As the evening drew on, the Signalman prepared his gear;
"sandwiches with cake, for you tonight my dear".
His wife looks on as her Railwayman dons his coat;
as moments from now he begins his journey to work - so remote.

The long lonely walk he knew so well;
how many walked the route, he couldn't tell.

The lonely Signal-Box stands beside the tracks;
exposed to all weathers, yet immune to gale attacks.

The night would bring another storm soon;
as up ahead the earie haze surrounds the Moon.
He leaves the path, climbs the steps of the Box;
in the distance, barks the hunting Fox.

The changing shift, of Signalmen like that;
normally a time to update and to chat.
But tonight, was different, as the other man hurries;
not wanting to stay, his heart full of worries.

And as he signs his name into the book;
The other man leaves without a backward look.
Alone now in this fortress bleak, he surveys the rural scene;
the Register, full of trains that passed, no visitors had been.

And so, his night shift starts again;
he deals with traffic, train by train.
The only sounds his ears can tell;
are those of Railway Telegraph, and bell.

He checked his fob-watch against Cabin clock;
the freight train passed, on route to distant Dock.
2 beats to the Box ahead, means 'Train on Line';
2-1 to box in rear, the line is clear and all is fine.

The gale outside matured now, interspersed with rain;
the Signalman he heard two beats, that suggest another train.
But there wasn't one due, the Signalman knew;
and he heard the two Black-5s before coming into view.

The Signalman greedily drained his coffee mug dry;
still thirsty though he knew not why.
And there from beneath the bridge of stone;

the charging double-headed train, proved he's not alone.

Two fire breathing Steam Dragons, convey their ten-coach train;
they thundered past the Signal-Box, along the track 'Up Main'.
He saw within the pool of light, as it roared and clattered past;
the ghostly, pleading wails, and spectral forms, held him frozen and aghast.

The shaken Bobby fought for breath as the tail light came along;
he thought he'd heard the bell's two beats, so surely can't be wrong.
In normal times he'd send two beats, and 2-1 to the rear;
but this time he was standing there, struck solid with the fear.

The train roared on relentlessly, returning to the night;
as the man tried to regain some sense, recovering from his fright.
Outside the Box the howling gale, perhaps the greatest storm;
and then beside the door outside, he thought he saw the form.

The ancient over hanging Oak, was struck by lightning with a crash;
the branch was hurled against the door, to sound a deadly thrash.
And then as though on pre-set tone, the storm was all blown out;
on seeing there, the old newsprint, he saw what brought this about.

A dozen years ago this night, the landslide took the train;
the hundred people and their train, were back to haunt again.

BY JACK D. HARRISON
17-01-2018

THE RAILWAY DEAD

I am that Signalman you knew;
who worked bell and levers day and night;
I met with a train whilst walking home;
but fell, and lost the light.

I'm the Platelayer who missed his 'Look-out';
who knew the Rules, and what they're all about.
The P-way Engineers took 'Possession;
but after 30 years, there's always one more lesson.

I'm the Driver of the Express Train;
who knew 'The Route', there and back again.
I didn't think they'd drop the stone;
from the urban bridge, but they ne'er atone.

And poor Jack Mills, they took your train;
you stood your ground and felt the pain.
That one dark night the Robbers struck;
stole two million, with no witness there to look.

And all too often in the early hours;
the Suicides jump beyond all our powers.
What malady brings this aberration?
that makes our Youth die, by the Station.

We are the 'Railway Dead', all free now from Sin;
we leave behind our 'Kith and kin'.
Thousands every year - such tragedy;
it's our job to recite their names - in loving memory.

BY JACK D. HARRISON
27 JANUARY-2018

SILENT WATCHERS

You came to visit, we who repose here;
we saw you pass by, and watched from windows,
oh, so near.

Pioneering treatment we had most weeks;
as threats to the public,
they just called us freaks.

When EEG had tried and then failed,
oh such was the anguish;
we wept and we wailed.
Of various ages, the young and the old;
we had the Lobotomy after shaving us bald

You visit our graveside and we wanted to speak;
to say "don't forget us, our lives were so bleak".
Even on bright sunny days in this sad, lonely place;
"We died here".

FOR THEM,
BY JACK D. HARRISON

THE END OF AN ERA

From 5-5-5 to 5-5-7;
the Railway telegraph sounded like Heaven.
The sounds of a Signalman's shift my dear;
filled boys of all ages with hope and cheer.

Hopes that they too would join the Railway;
to follow Dads or Uncles was the traditional way.
From GWR or LMS to British Rail;
Beeching's axe was beyond the pale.

That murderer of Branch Railways;
had no respect for long gone days.
His bitter pill for Rural Halts;
was over-kill, for their little faults.

From Westleigh & Bedford, and Alnwick to Cornhill;
The news of their decline, I've fair had my fill.

And the loss of poor little Wyre line;
announced the start of Fleetwood's decline.

I loved every shift there, a pleasurable toil;
sending train after train down, from Chlorine to Oil.
I moan for our Heritage in every debate;
but where was Wyre Council, as usual, too late.

And now as the time comes for Electrification;
they've smashed all my Boxes, with some jubilation.
So now at the end as I tell unto thee;
there's just one Box left, that's Poulton No 3.

BY JACK D. HARRISON
TUES 16-01-2018

Sadly, the last traditional (Lever frame) signal box was allowed to be demolished, with apparently, no attempt by Local Authorities to save or preserve any of it.

JDH- FEBRUARY-2018.

TIMES PAST;

AND

MORE GENERAL

POETRY

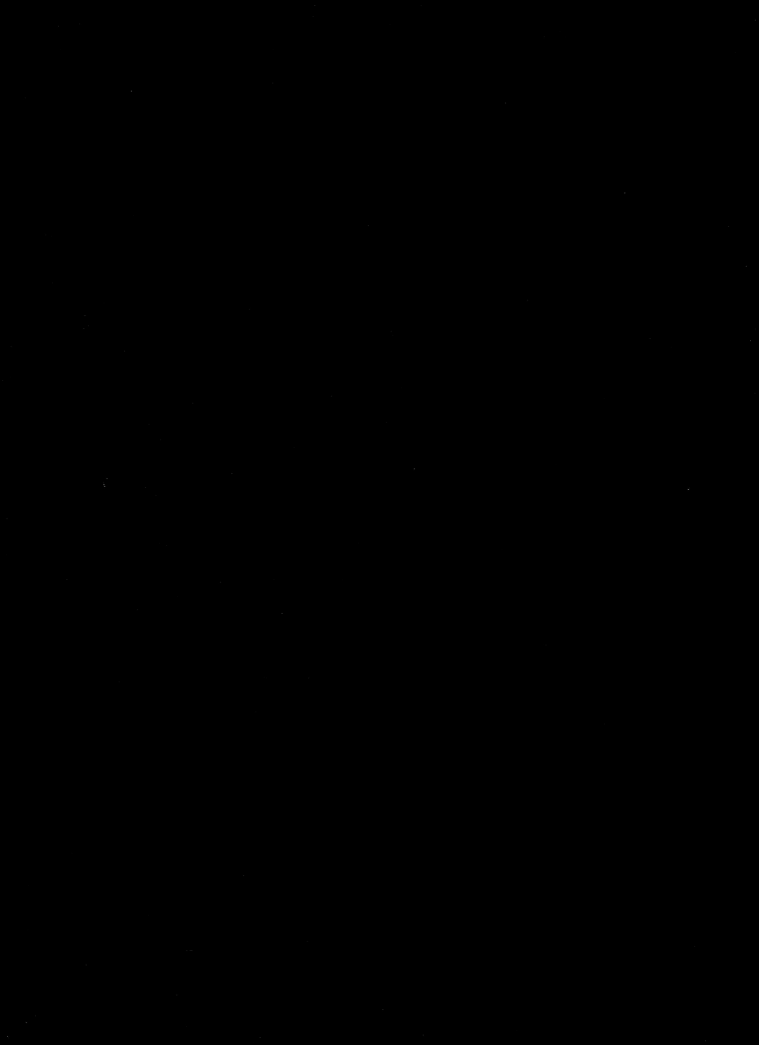

A VISION OF FLEETWOOD

A boat like a 'Skiff', or a 'Smack' as you see;
awaiting three children, all running with glee.
The place was old Fleetwood, an eon ago;
the Granddad would greet them, and off they would go.

"A-Fishing, A-fishing", they called out to Granddad;
to miss out on the trip, they'd have to be mad.
"A typical Port like Fleetwood"? I hear,
Oh, there's nothing quite typical, living here, year by year

The town was established in 1836;
between Sea and the river, between and betwixt.
In pleasanter times they sailed everywhere;
ships like Reciprocity, had carried her wares.

She carried her cargo right into Skipool;
with a hold full of corn, from perhaps Liverpool.
Her Master, Great Granddad, Cptn Peter Harrison;
he supplied local Commerce, with goods to thrive upon.

And so, as we look on the image with this;
it's nice to look back, and again reminisce
A vision of children, with a boat like a Dory;
reminds us of Fleetwood's past Maritime glory.

BY JACK D. HARRISON
DEC-2017

BLUEBELLS

Bluebells ring out the coming Spring;
with promises of longer days to bring.
Of warmer times to venture out;
And witness new life, all about.

Beneath a hundred woodland canopies;
the ranks of blue, surround our picnic delicacies.
To and fro, their breeze blown heads;
Support the spider's silken threads.

A patch of blue amongst the green;
Creating new sights, never seen.
Hues of blue to lift the heart;
Precedes the Summer, yet to start.

And as you walk the stream doth flow;
You're not to pick the Bluebells, as you know.
Just look in awe, at the springtime feast;
Don't make them another species, now deceased.

BY JACK D. HARRISON
2017-18.

CASTLES ON THE BEACH

The children pause to view their toil;
as relentless tide awaits to spoil.
Remembering as they float to sleep;
their seaside castle, with sturdy Keep.

Another day with bucket and spade;
their work's the pride of the Esplanade.
With castle moat and battlement;
they dig yet more, and ne'er relent.

Old Fleetwood Town is safe again;
with defences from the Sea.
The labour of another season;
built with child-like glee.

They break to eat another goodie;
Rimmer's Vimto, or parched brown peas.
They never think of new generations;
but in later life, there's much veneration.

Industrious to a fault these diggers;
shifting sand with whoops and sniggers.
Who can build the highest tower?
the largest Castle brings more power.

And can they beat the coming tide;
to be the best, they raced and vied.
Late afternoons and early evenings;
racing sunsets, and all they bring.

Thus, are Fleetwood holidays spent;
sunny days they came and went.
And so, to beds the children reach;
then dream of castles;
on a Fleetwood beach.

BY JACK D. HARRISON. 24-3-2018. ©

A FLEETWOOD SUNSET

A moody sky surrounds old Sol,
as he takes his evening rest;
The tide retreats along the beach;
no longer at its zest.

Four billion years have seen this sight,
along these changing shores.
It happened long before we came,
to call them 'ours or yours'.

What makes such hues to merge, perfuse,
the orange and the yellows?
What is it, causes light to change;
and make our evenings mellow?

As boys play on the sandy beach,
and wonder "what's out there"?
The passing ferry sails along;
as though without a care.

And so, the scene continues on,
the setting Sun retires.
as strollers on the lower Prom;
observe the Solar fires.

Two billion years our galaxy's yet to see;
I wonder if old Fleetwood town,
Will still remain, to be.
Or will the Sea reclaim the land,
Long after you and me?

And will the future strollers have, a reason to regret;
One last evening coastal stroll;
And a final Fleetwood Sunset?

BY JACK D. HARRISON
24-3-2018 ©

DIESEL DRAGONS

Long ago, in a Galaxy far away;
Diesel Locos roamed the 'Permanent-Way'.
With passing arrows on BR Blue;
it really happened, I'm not kidding you.

Their horns sang aloud like this and that;
I even herd one sing ***"On Ilkley Moor ba'tat"***.
They ruled the Rails smelling high with diesel;
no time for any EMU Weasel.

At Loco Depots the did reside;
they spread their glory nationwide.
But sad to say they rule no more;
the 40s, Peaks, and many more.

So, drink a glass of Diesel Juice;
as smoky breaths they do produce.
Electric Trains are clean they say;
I'd rather have the same old way.

BY JACK D. HARRISON
2017-18

THE FLASHBACKS

Day turns to night, and night turns to day;
as the Flashback comes in the same old way.
Catching the survivor unaware;
it's there in my face, without a care.

Whether as 'Day-mare', or 'Nightmare';
there is no reprieve, and again I despair.
It's vivid and scary, and oh so real;
but at least on my own, no tears will reveal.

The routine is shared by so many of us;
except for the detail, that's so horrendous.
Unannounced it sneaks like a viper;
or lands like a bogeyman, making me hyper.

I'm driving along the green country lane;
then the Drink-driver's THERE; all over again.
On my side of the road, incredibly drunk;
I slam the wheel over, towards the tree-trunk.

I saved a few inches, to bring him down the side;
my car was ripped open, there's nowhere to hide.
He smashed my rear axle, to rupture fuel tank;
But I'm still in one piece, wondering who, do I thank.

I'm OK when driving, a pass-time that helps;
but through the long nights, no-one hears my yelps.
It's been twenty-five years, since that awful event;
and still it can scare, no way for it to vent.

The door in the car with me, or the glass in my face;
or the horrible sound, in whichever place.
But I'm not a Victim, that's pathetic to me;
I'm a born Survivor, when it's midnight, or three.

BY JACK D. HARRISON. 31-03-2018. ©

FLEETWOOD FOLK HURRAH

(To the old Confederate tune of 'Bonny Blue Flag')

VERSE 1
Two hundred years, and more ago, the berths of Skipool creek;
all rang with the sounds of Commerce, working through the week.
With tallow from Old Russia, and timber from the North,
The ships up the Wyre boys, set sail and ventured forth.

CHORUS
Hoorah, Hurrah, we're Fleetwood folk we are;
hurrah for the Fleetwood folk, no better here or far.

VERSE 2
In 1836 my friends, the Fleetwood of our heart;
Sir Peter Hesketh's noble dream, would get a Royal start.
The Architect Sir Decimous, had planned the streets so well;
like spokes on a wheel they ran, so grand it was to tell.

CHORUS
Hoorah, Hurrah, we're Fleetwood folk we are;
hurrah for the Fleetwood folk, no better here or far.

VERSE 3
Once Railwaymen and fishermen, and Cargo carriers too;
we sailed all the seven seas, and off to places new.
In sailing Barques and Schooners, and fishing Smacks as well;
we grew our economy, and others, who can tell?

VERSE 4
But now in decline, we find the shipping has all gone;
with only our memories, and hopes to dream upon.

The fishing grounds are closed to us, and cargo routes have changed;
decisions that control us now, are clearly all deranged.

CHORUS
Hoorah, Hurrah, we're Fleetwood folk we are;
hurrah for the Fleetwood folk, no better here or far.
Hoorah, Hurrah, we're Fleetwood folk we are;
hurrah for the Fleetwood folk, no better here or far.

BY JACK D. HARRISON
SEPTEMBER 14-2018
(Jack's Birthday)

I COUNT THE HOURS

I lay here all alone, wishing you would come back home;
And the nights get ever longer without you.
Well I'm sorry that we fought, and to cause you so much pain;
All I want is to be with you again.

VERSE 2

Now I walk the same old paths, thinking of the aftermath;
And remember all the good times that we had.
But it's not the same alone, tell me how I can atone;
all I do is count the hours, that you've been gone.

VERSE 3

It seems just like yesterday, since you cried and ran away;
I'm so sorry that I did all that to you.
But I know in the end, you were more than just my friend;
please come back so we're together once again.

END CHORUS

Oh I count the silent hours every night and every day;
So many hours since you went away.
I count the seconds every hour without you;
I'd like to change this point of view.

BY JACK HARRISON 2018. ©

MESSAGE FROM HERCULANEUM

As you search and look upon my ancient bones, what do you think and discover? What do you learn of Marcus, the 10-year-old boy, who's scorched body, lays before you, still embracing the remains of my faithful pet dog; to provide a time capsule; telling what fate befell us on that awful day at Herculaneum, in 79AD.

My Father was a rich and successful trader of wine, olive oil and other imports from across our Roman Empire, which ensured the future of our growing town. Coming from such a family, boys like us did not have to work like others my age, so I had a live-in Tutor, who shared the other household slave quarters.

After lessons that day, I had played the usual games with my dog, and other boys in the atrium, until the tremors became more violent and prolonged. Then Mother and Father led us into the vaults by the shore, because it was thought to be a safe place to hide from the clouds of ash and other material. We had felt the tremors for years, and had not panicked before. My parents and grandparents knew of these tremors and were not unduly afraid.

By 01.00 AM the murmurs in the vault had settled down, as about 40 of us, family, slaves and various neighbours began to sleep as best we could. But suddenly, we were all awaken by a pulse of wind and heat, which blasted into our refuge [the vault], covering us all in thick, choking ash; making it impossible for most to breath. The abrasive dust tearing and destroying the lungs of victims.

We had watched the mountain of Vesuvius erupt in a huge mushroom cloud towards Pompei, which seemed to boil and march like a dreadful Legion, sometimes white, and then black. Yet still, we thought that we had escaped the fate of our neighbouring town. Most people had not even realised that it was a volcano, covered as it was for many years in lush green vegetation.

But then our 2,000yr old night began, as another pulse of wind and heat killed us all. In a moment, the searing heat removed all signs of life, and fluid and flesh, as my boyhood skull exploded; my charred skeleton distorted by the action of heat, more than a thousand degrees C.
18 hours after the mountain erupted, our town of 4,000 citizens, slaves and tradesmen, was removed from the face of the earth. Covered in 25m of Ash pumice, and volcanic and other debris for you to find - and convey this boy's message, from poor Herculaneum.

BY JACK D. HARRISON
21-08-2018

OUR WOLVES IN SUMMER

It may come as some surprise;
that dogs don't come in s 'one-fit' size.
One can't drag dogs on marathons;
just because they're 'keep-fit morons'.

And on these Summer days of heat;
The beach is full of dogs who meet.
Comparing notes on owners who;
do walk their dogs, until black and blue.

One German Shepherd needs the shade;
loves to dream of youthful escapade.
Whilst an upstart young and fiery Russel;
likes to run around, all full of muscle.

It's not about huge walks and mileage;
We must remember health and their age.
Some dogs like to enjoy life;
Helping pushy owners, through their strife.

Our wolves aren't dumb, we all should know;
some 'walkies times', they may not want to go.
It's far too hot beneath our paws;
It'll overheat, and make us sore.

We'd love to go, when Sun goes down;
along leafy lane, or through the town.
We do not want to make you mean;
But your playful pup, is now sixteen.

BY JACK D. HARRISON
(June-2018)

PERFECT SYMETRY

Two examples of perfect Symmetry;
captured in this summer imagery.
Delicate as they both can be;
their indelible hues, for all to see.

And so, upon that Summer day;
the insect approaches in the usual way.
The gentle breeze, a breath so light;
affects the Butterfly in flight.

It sees the flower, its Landing Zone;
as all around the Honey Bees drone.
Like a plane and a Carrier ship;
the Butterfly lands, with such Airmanship.

Both threatened by evil pesticide;
such damage does it do inside.
We must protect this annual show;
provider of that warming glow.

The Butterfly, flower, and leaves of green;
for millions of years have er'er been seen.
How can we dare to threaten this?
fair products, of Sun, seed and chrysalis.

BY JACK D. HARRISON
11-01-2018
(Inspired by a Photo by Steven Speed).

SIGHTLESS FIGURES

What do they see, with their timeless eyes;
three lonely figures, gaze upon restless Skies.
Who do they yearn for, out there in the blue?
why, husbands and Daddies, the Port miss them too.

They sailed out last night as Fleetwood still slept;
those statues tell everything, and oh, how they wept.
The docks are now silent, betrayed by 'Outsiders;
our Heritage denied, and not by Sea-siders.

A baby with Mother, along with a young girl;
unseeing eyes weep a tear, like salty pearl.
Flowers for their Trawlerman, to see him off safe;
but he never returned, swallowed up by a wave.

So, the Statues remain there, and weather the storms;
their kin and their menfolk, upon the Sea roams.
Oh. people of Fleetwood, is this how it ends?
sightless figures by the Coast, too late for amends.

BY JACK D. HARRISON
DEC-2017

SLEEPY SHEPHERD

When daily toils of work enable;
then just climb up and claim a table.
Dream away your puppy life;
Don't let those Targets rule your life.

Thoughts of biscuits, and of bones;
forget the laptops and the phones.
The World will pass, and all its troubles;
your dreams like thoughts, in little bubbles.

German Shepherd look at you;
purple lead and collar new.
The office noise, drones on and on;
as you recall Tchaikovsky No 1. *

Puppy, puppy, don't you care;
your little pads show you're a 'Long Hair'.
Mostly black with feet of tan;
you'll bowl them over, as only you can.

And When he grows, just like a bear;
his big black fur gets everywhere.
He'll come in close demanding cuddles;
wash your face, leave you all of a muddle.

BY JACK D. HARRISON
06-11-2917

Refers to Tchaikovsky Piano Concerto No. 1, 2nd Movement.
Puppy music if ever there was one.

SPEARS OVER THE WYRE

Spears of light upon the river;
a message from Zeus, to make us shiver.
As Moon and tide cover the sands;
the Sea surrounds our ancient lands.

The clouds are pierced with the solar light;
our star reached down with all its might.
And as the lonely, warbling Curlews;
marks the passing time and views.

Views of silent river there;
tells the tale of Fleetwood, where.
The ancient Mariners plied our shore;
but now to Skipool they sail no more.

BY JACK D. HARRISON

THE KESTREL

The loveliest voice that anyone heard;
from that noble Engine, the Kestrel bird.
Swooping at speed through Rose Bay Willow;
or hovering at stations, a proud looking fellow.

Born in 1967, and a SULTER by breed,
with 4,000Hp, it's a beast made for speed.
The hues of yellow, chocolate, and white;
you'll know when she passes, oh heck what a sight.

Her birthplace at Loughborough, so special and rare;
as no further orders would be generated there.
But alas there would be no happy reunion;
for she ended her days in the Soviet Union.

BY JACK D. HARRISON
22-01-2018

I KNEW THEM

One evening there, in mid-July;
as Solar warmth still blessed the sky.
I lay and dozed amidst the garden's shade;
and ruminated how the world was made.

Across the ocean of my dream;
over mountains and lake that gleam.
I flew through skies, without a cloud
and touched the nightly starry shroud.

In the moonlit glade, beneath the leafy canopy;
I saw them, radiant as any light can be.
Without foreboding, or hint of fear;
heeding their telepathic call, "Draw near".
I knew them!

Our Visitors as in some Galactic verse;
returning to Earth, they transverse the Universe.

100 million lightyears from door to door;
a dozen Quasars they did see, and maybe more.

They had no need of ship, known to me;
their form, translucent, was pure Energy.
Yet fear not I, to be amongst them;
born of the stars ourselves;
as Life-forms of the day and night - and Elves.
I knew them.

You see my friends.
When stars grow old and die, to Super Nova;
their heavy elements blast all over.
Lightspeed, across the infinite;
endless journeys for some- and YET..

Some elements land on an infant Earth;
colliding Comets, deposit water within her girth.
Therefore, with Chemistry, Space and Time;
'Children of the Stars', is not so crazy a line.

And so, we have this meeting in the glade;
beneath the cool and quiet Moonlight shade.
This poem now done, no more to advance;
unlike the Constellations in their nightly dance.

If you're still reading this, then pull over;
The poem's about to go 'Hypernova'.

BY JACK D. HARRISON
SUMMER-2017

THE SEA SHALL COME AGAIN

A younger Fleetwood, in 1927
lost its grasp of Peace and Heaven;
the Sea came crashing over the coast
vulnerable all, who knew WHO, got it most.

Residents devastated, and made to shiver;
a mass of water, from Sea to River.
Dead cattle, debris and Railway sleepers;
roamed the streets, just like Grim Reapers.

The mark outside the Strawberry Gardens;
shows that Nature rarely ever pardons.
Stained indelible, in our history;
would it return? remained (for them), a mystery.

But then again after fifty years;
the Sea returned and brought more tears.
A South West wind and high Spring tide;
brought chaos over, Fleetwood wide.

Again, the Sea crossed to the Wyre;
forcing people to flee much higher.
The damage caused around the town;
would bring some thoughts of Christmas, down.

The sea-drowned worms, disgusting things;
resembling scattered bits of string.
Around that weekend, we watched and waited;
volunteered and worked, un-abated.

And now in 2017, the new Defence Works daily seen;
Passing again, safe through this Anniversary time.
We people of Fleetwood, speak the same refrain;
Deep down we know, "The Sea shall come again",

BY JACK D. HARRISON
11-11-2017

THE SHORT CUT

There's a cheeky wee spider, in my bed;
that's why I'm mad.
The wolf jumps up to say, "Can I have some too Dad"?

It could have had the whole place,
to roam as he did please;
but no, he chose my bloody bed, to wander and to tease.

He could have put the kettle on, and made us bread and cheese;
but no, he crossed my only bed;
a short cut if you please.

JACK D. HARRISON
01.50hrs. 20-6-18

Rob Callighan

THE VIEW ACROSS THE RIVER

The view across the river there,
across the river Wyre;
It took me back so far in time,
and thus, inspired the Rhyme.

It could be 18-something there,
another World from this;
My mind could see the sailing ships,
and times of 'Schooner Bliss'.

And then I saw another view,
out there, across the river;

to times of youth and happiness,
that made me start to shiver.

That view across the Wyre, there
with relics of the rolling Sea;
The lifebelts, quay and sandbanks there;
bring those memories home to thee.

BY JACK D. HARRISON
SAT: 27-01-2018

THE TAUNT OF THE DRUNK DRIVERS

We are the DRUNK DRIVERS, and your MURDERERS! Saw ye our DEEDS?
Heard ye the scream of our MINDLESS CHARGES in the night, and the shuddering crashes?
Saw ye our work by the roadside, the shrouded things lying,
Moaning to God that He made them - the maimed and the dying?
Husbands or sons, WIVES or DAUGHTERS - AND SURVIVORS!; we break them. We are the DRUNKS!

WE ARE THE DRUNK DRIVERS AND YE SERVE US. HOW DARE YOU INNOCENTS GROW WEARY;
UNSTEADY AT NIGHT-TIME, AT NOON-TIME; OR WAKING, WHEN CLOUDED MIND MEETS A NEW DAY.
OUT ON THE ROADS AND LANES, WE WAIT FOR THE HOUR OF 'OPENING';
AND THE TIME OF SLAUGHTER ON OUR ROADS.

WE ARE THE DRUNK DRIVERS AND WE HURT YOU, THERE ON THE TARMAC WAYS;
SCREENED AND PROTECTED BY A LENIENT JUDICERY.
ATTENDING AA MEETINGS TO PACIFY THE OUTRAGE.
OUR APPEAL RETURNS THE LICENSE TO KILL, TO MAIME AND CHANGE LIVES.
HAVING NO CONSCIENCE, WHAT CARE WE FOR THE BLUE-LIGHT SERVICES;
WHO HAVE TO DEAL WITH OUR DEEDS, WITH SUCH ENDURING STOICISM.

WE ARE THE DRUNK DRIVERS, AND WE TAUNT YOU.

By Jack D. Harrison
2017-18

Composed in the spirit of the great Poem written by Gilbert Frankau called '*The Voice of the Guns*', 1916.
NB- Original in lower case, then I join my poem (*Taunt of the Drunk Drivers*), in Upper case. Left in Upper case to reflect my rage.

WE ARE THE WRITERS

We are 'The Writers'.
Witness of Time and History;
constructing lines of Verse, and Prose;
and Mystery.

Describing our thoughts, our lives;
and Environment.
Writing of Fleetwood, the Sea;
and things to lament.

From Plato and Socrates;
to Owen and Sassoon.
We follow their calling;
on a wet afternoon.
We are 'The Writers'.

JACK D. HARRISON
02-11-2017 AD

THE OLD BABUSHKA

Old Babushka far away;
working on the Railway.
Through Siberian winter snow;
making trains depart and go.

Wrapped and shaped like a 'Christmas Pud';
swing that pick, I knew you could.
We see you through the train window;
your rosy face and cheeks aglow.

"Dobre Din" old rounded grandma;
work and toil your life away.
Your youth was filled with Red Guard
days. Party member in the usual way.

Tell us tales of the Revolution;
how it toughened your constitution.
How you stood with Lenin that night;
how vodka flowed until first light.

Shifting ballast from dawn to night.
work and work, true Stakhanovite.
And so, Babushka, old you are;
Come, take your fill from the Samovar.

BY JACK D. HARRISON
01-09-2018

AN OLD LITERARY FRIEND

I am that writer you knew my friend;
but I had to go on, to pages new;
with a lifetime's packing still to do.

Remember, how in the long dark and lonely nights,
we exchanged our news, views and poetry?

How we passed the time, wondering if this or that would rhyme;
we knew the true quality of each other's work.
One shared a joke or stifled tear;
wishing when, and would, the dawn, draw near.

And though I can no longer write;
I try to visit, and watch you composing through the night.

How you work and toil with pen or key;
to achieve a finished poem.
That's 'Literary Alchemy',
live, and in action.
No sense of doubt, no remorse, not a fraction.

And if we had our time again,
what issues would we mend?
What would I change of world or self,
to better comprehend?

But one thing e'er remains,
and on this you can depend.
However long I here repose;
I'm still, your old Literary friend.

BY JACK D. HARRISON
00.00HRS 09-10-2018

AUTUMN

BY CHRISTOPHER LUKE

As green leaves turn to rust and gold
And fall silently from the tree
All at once I feel rather old
More so too, today, as my senses take leave of me!

As the days shorten and nights lengthen
In preparation for the winter season ahead
One is reminded of how quickly time passes
As we no sooner appear born before we're dead!

As another year draws swiftly to a close
And crops are gathered in at Harvest time
I find myself looking back at months and years already gone
And fretfully ahead, wondering what lies in store much further down the line.

As one bids a fond "Auf Wiedersehen" to the summer sun
And laments the passing of loved friends and past times long gone
One is mindful that few things stay the same
Before they too vanish from the naked eye.

Betwixt thanksgiving at Harvest and the expectation of Christmas
The solemnity of Armistice Day reminds one too
Of unsung heroes and long-forgotten sons
Lost in war and frequently ignored amidst the passage of time.

As rustic leaves fall from the trees
Leaving branches bare once more
Their natural apparel fills the ground
Like clothes once worn, now lie strewn across, a child's bedroom floor.

And so, today, as the weather turns that much colder
One instantly feels somewhat older
No longer the boy I once was attired in my grey school shorts
As one earnestly seeks warmer climates in far-flung ports.

God bless you and yours this Autumn. Hope to see you soon.
With love, as always,

© CHRISTOPHER LUKE
21 November 2017

THE WAY TO PLANET X

Far out on the edge of what we know;
the strange orbits of Oort Cloud objects dost go.

The realm of 'Goblins', and other Plutoids lies;
as new distant objects meet our telescopic eyes.
the existence of 'Planet X', our past knowledge defies;
discovered by 'Mauna Kea'? under bright Pacific skies.

To find new lands has always been 'The Human Way';
As Astronomers did, this October day.
To pass the light of understanding;
And find new neighbours, quite astounding.

Far smaller than our homely Earth;
barely 300 km around its lonely girth.
The tiny 'Goblin', leads the way;
to lands remote, and a whole new day.

BY JACK D. HARRISON
Poet/Author
02-10-2018. ©

Thank you Readers, for having a look;
upon my latest Poetry book.
I hope you found something to cheer;
to help you through the night and day in here.

The last page and final lines,
are not the end of happier times.
I hope like me, you find the will;
To work your mind, and use the quill.
Tis mightier than any sword.

Sincerely.

Jack D. Harrison
Poet/Author

ACKNOWLEDGEMENTS

Taylor Crowshaw.
Christopher Luke.
JoJo.
Rob Calligan.
Geoffrey Plant.
Steven Speed.
Owners, Moderators and Readers, Photographic and other contributors and followers of the 'Fleetwood Past and Present Facebook page.
The Production Team and everyone involved in my books at AuthorHouse Publishers.

My apologies to anyone I may have left out, but I assure you, I am grateful for all of your inspiration, help, input, and encouragement. Thank you **everyone.**

Jack D. Harrison.
Poet/Author.

ABOUT THE AUTHOR

JACK D. HARRISON has had a very varied background. He was a Railway Signalman between 1978 and 1988, when he had to retire early following an injury at work. Then in 1993, a drunk driver caused further injuries, and since then, he has had to re-invent himself several times; but this process has helped in several ways. It certainly helped to provide more time for his creative tendencies and he does not do idleness very well. He likes the peace and freedom of living alone, but he also enjoys the company of others, at times.

Jack has always liked writing since boyhood. Now with this third book, he thinks that it became addictive. Whilst some of his work is based upon his own experiences, he can also write about a wide range of material and genre; and his books include Verse and Prose. His first book **'Rhyming Lines'** was all poetry with a small amount of song lyrics. Book 2 **'Memoirs of a Signalman'** as suggested, tells of his years on the Railway; probably his most favourite time. Jack has also spent time as a British Legion Case Worker; which greatly added to his knowledge of the Armed Forces, Veterans, and related issues.

Sometimes he writes about a particular idea or project, but other times he can be inspired by an image or person's situation, and he stays with it, to see where it takes him. To other budding Poet/Authors out there, Jack would recommend staying with the idea, rather than putting it aside for tomorrow, or another time. The problem is, the same idea may be lost, or it may appear quite different.

At the time of writing this current book, he also worked on plans for a fourth project. So, it is fair to say that he could be becoming Prolific. More news about his fourth project will follow soon. But either way, Jack has always been proud of the fact that many readers have told him that his work-" *touches their lives*", and that much of his Poetry actually "*tells stories*".

Printed in the United States
By Bookmasters